Winter
A Folio Anthology

Winter
A Folio Anthology

EDITED BY

Sue Bradbury

INTRODUCED BY

Susan Cooper

ILLUSTRATED BY

Petra Börner

London
The Folio Society
2016

Published by The Folio Society Ltd
44 Eagle Street, London WC1R 4FS
www.foliosociety.com

Selection © The Folio Society 2016

Introduction © Susan Cooper 2016
Illustrations © Petra Börner 2016

Typeset at The Folio Society in Caslon.
Printed on Abbey Pure Rough paper at L.E.G.O. S.p.A.,
Vicenza, Italy, and bound by them in quarter cloth
with Modigliani paper sides printed with
a design by the artist

SUE BRADBURY became Editorial Director of The Folio Society in 1984, a post she held for twenty-five years. Her own publications include *Midnight Madonna* (1995), a novel set in the Spanish Civil War, the biography *Joanna, George and Henry: A Pre-Raphaelite Tale of Art, Love and Friendship* (2012), a translation of *Three Tragedies* by Federico Garcia Lorca, and she also collaborated with Robert Fox on his magisterial four-volume *Eyewitness to History* for the Folio Society. She was awarded the OBE in 2010 for services to the publishing industry.

SUSAN COOPER has written for theatre and television but is best-known as an author of books for children and young adults. Her five-book sequence *The Dark is Rising* won the Newbery Medal, a Newbery Honor and two Carnegie Honour Awards, and is published in a Folio edition. Her most recent novel is *Ghost Hawk*. Susan Cooper lives in the United States, where she has received the American Library Association's lifetime Margaret A. Edwards Award for 'a significant and lasting contribution to young adult literature'.

PETRA BÖRNER, originally from Sweden, is an artist and illustrator based in London. She studied Fashion at St Martins in London, and her first commissions came from *Elle* and *Vogue*. Her client list now includes the V&A, Heal's and publishers Random House, Penguin and Bloomsbury. Her work has been exhibited worldwide, at the National Portrait Gallery, Claire de Rouen, the Design Museum in London, C/O Illustration in Stockholm and the Swedish Embassy in Tokyo.

The trees are leafless and the flowers have died, taking all colour with them. The days grow short, the nights cold, the skies a gloomy grey – but then, one dark winter's day, the firſt snowflakes flicker down, and they fall and fall until the world is transformed, gleaming, silent, magical.

Those are the two faces of winter, filling this little book. For writers at the top of the Northern Hemisphere, the season that ends and begins the year is a time either of harshness or of enchantment. It has always ruled their lives, as it rules ours, through the dwindling days until the winter solſtice, the shorteſt day, when gradually light begins once more to defeat darkness, with the promise of life re-awakened.

Your chance of winter bringing ferocious cold or furious ſtorm depends on where and when you live. Winters were colder in Britain between the sixteenth and nineteenth centuries, the time known as the Little Ice Age. Henry VIII is said to have ridden his horse down the frozen Thames to Greenwich, and the ice was thick enough to support recurrent Froſt Fairs like the one celebrated by John Evelyn in 1684: 'All sorts of trades and shops furnished ... even to a printing press, where the people and ladies took a fancy to have their names printed, and the day and year set down when printed on the Thames.' But the last Frost Fair was in 1814, and today's London has seen a properly white Christmas only four times in the last half-century. In Robert Frost's woods in the north-east of the United States, winter is colder, snowier and much longer, and a daffodil unwise enough to poke up its head in February may be under deep snow in late March.

Christmas is the warm heart of winter, of course: a religious festival wise enough to embrace echoes, from the days when primitive man's response to the shortest day was to lure back the light with sacrifice and ritual. Its name dates from the fourth century, when the Christian church chose to celebrate the birth of Christ on December 25th – a day that was already the birthday of the sun-god Mithras, whose worship had spread northward through the Roman Empire. Candles, gifts and evergreens are echoes from earlier ages too, even though it was the Victorians who planted the Christmas tree in our year.

Most of us – like the poets Dylan Thomas and Leonard Clark – remember moments of childhood Christmas with aching clarity. Though my American grandchildren hang their Christmas stockings over the fireplace, in my English childhood we hung ours at the end of the bed, and the quintessential seasonal magic was the moment of waking up to feel a weight over your feet, and to know that it was Christmas morning and that presents – ideally, a book, in those book-starved days of World War Two – had spilled out of the stocking. Does that hope of words on the printed page still survive in today's happily acquisitive small stocking-openers, I wonder, or do they dream only of electronic devices with small screens?

Perhaps the most heartbreaking of all Christmas memories dates back to World War One, involving doomed young men who were not many years away from their own childhood. It's the moment in 1914 recalled here by a German officer, when suddenly soldiers from both sides of the line began exchanging chocolate and cigarettes, and eventually, astonishingly, playing a game of football. The game lasted for an hour, and finished 'with a score of three goals to two in favour of Fritz against Tommy' – and then, next morning, the war took over again from the spell of Christmas, and they were all back at the business of trying to kill each other.

Even today, after the warmth of Christmas celebration fades, we find ourselves back in the icy grasp of winter, for even longer than we had been before. But then New Year's Day passes, and the days grow longer; though snow falls and icicles hang by the wall, sooner or later the first green shoot will break through the frozen ground.

If winter is the season of darkness and death, so too it holds the promise of bright rebirth, as our planet swings and brings back the precious emotion called hope. The best thing about winter isn't the magical snowflake, or the delight of Christmas, or the magnificence of storm. It's the fact that we know it's going to be followed by spring.

SUSAN COOPER

Winter
A Folio Anthology

Stopping by Woods on a
Snowy Evening

Whose woods these are I think I know.
His house is in the village, though;
He will not see me stopping here
To watch his woods fill up with snow.

My little horse must think it queer
To stop without a farmhouse near
Between the woods and frozen lake
The darkest evening of the year.

He gives his harness bells a shake
To ask if there is some mistake.
The only other sound's the sweep
Of easy wind and downy flake.

The woods are lovely, dark, and deep,
But I have promises to keep,
And miles to go before I sleep,
And miles to go before I sleep.

Robert Frost

From the tenth day of the Twelfth Month it snowed very heavily, and the other ladies-in-waiting gathered large quantities of snow and heaped it in lids; then we decided to build a real snow mountain in the garden. Having summoned the servants, we told them it was on Her Majesty's orders, so they all got to work. Men from the Office of Grounds, who had come to do some sweeping, also joined in, and soon the mountain was rising high above the ground. Next came some officials from the Office of the Empress's Household, who made suggestions and helped build an especially beautiful mountain. There were also a few Assistant Officials from the Emperor's Private Office and some more men from the Office of Grounds, so that soon we had about twenty people working away. In addition messages were sent to the servants of duty, saying that a special stipend would be given to anyone who helped on that day, but that those who did not appear for work could expect nothing. This brought the men rushing out, except for those who lived far away and could not be informed.

When the mountain was finished, officials from the Office of the Empress's Household were summoned and given rolls of silk, tied up in sets of two. They threw the rolls on to the veranda, and each of the workmen came and took a set.

From *The Pillow Book of Sei Shonagon*,
translated by Ivan Morris

The ground was hard, the air was ſtill, my road was lonely: I walked faſt till I got warm, and then I walked slowly to enjoy and to analyse the species of pleasure brooding for me in the hour and situation. It was three o'clock; the church bell tolled as I passed under the belfry: the charm of the hour lay in its approaching dimness, in the low-gliding and pale-beaming sun. I was a mile from Thornfield, in a lane noted for wild roses in summer, for nuts and blackberries in autumn, and even now possessing a few coral treasures in hips and haws, but whose beſt winter delight lay in its utter solitude and leafless repose. If a breath of air ſtirred, it made no sound here; for there was not a holly, not an evergreen to ruſtle, and the ſtripped hawthorn and hazel bushes were as ſtill as the white worn ſtones which causewayed the middle of the path. Far and wide, on each side, there were only fields, where no cattle now browsed; and the little brown birds, which ſtirred occasionally in the hedge, looked like single russet leaves that had forgotten to drop.

Charlotte Brontë, from *Jane Eyre*

A 14-Year-Old Convalescent Cat
in the Winter

I want him to have another living summer,
to lie in the sun and enjoy the *douceur de vivre* –
because the sun, like golden rum in a rummer,
is what makes an idle cat *un tout petit peu ivre* –

I want him to lie stretched out, contented,
revelling in the heat, his fur all dry and warm,
an Old Age Pensioner, retired, resented
by no one, and happinesses in a beelike swarm

to settle on him – postponed for another season
that last fated hateful journey to the vet
from which there is no return (and age the reason),
which must come soon – as I cannot forget.

Gavin Ewart

As we search among the vegetable plots for fuel, I pause at the Brussels sprouts. They are beautiful with their tight fists of sprouts bunched up at the ftalks, and the long-ftemmed leaves curving all round the plants. I wonder why so few people remark their beauty. They look like a sculptor's work. The vegetables mature as the flower garden withers. Purple sprouting broccoli thickens and throws out its rich, blue-green foliage; banked rows of celery thrive in the frofts, each plant encased, for blanching, in newspaper and ftring. Leeks ftand upright in their severe carved folds, rushing up to flower before we are ready to pull them. There is so much to be done in the garden juft now. We wonder if we shall manage it before the winter frofts clamp down the earth, making all work impossible.

Clare Leighton, from *Four Hedges:*
A Gardener's Chronicle

And in the frosty season, when the sun
Was set, and visible for many a mile
The cottage windows through the twilight blazed,
I heeded not the summons: happy time
It was indeed for all of us – to me
It was a time of rapture! Clear and loud
The village clock tolled six, – I wheeled about,
Proud and exulting like an untired horse
That cares not for its home. All shod with steel,
We hissed along the polished ice in games
Confederate, imitative of the chase
And woodland pleasures, – the resounding horn,
The pack loud bellowing, and the hunted hare.
So through the darkness and the cold we flew,
And not a voice was idle; with the din,
Meanwhile, the precipices rang aloud;
The leafless trees and every icy crag
Tinkled like iron;
While the distant hills
Into the tumult sent an alien sound
Of melancholy not unnoticed, while the stars
Eastward were sparkling clear, and in the west
The orange of the evening died away.

William Wordsworth, from *The Prelude*

8

Older children told stories about pump handles and kids who put their tongues on them. You put your tongue on a pump handle when it's so bitterly cold, the spit freezes, you're stuck there. Then either they pull you away, ripping your tongue off, or else pitch a tent over you and wait for spring and hope for the best. It scared us little kids, the thought that one day during recess we might forget and put our tongue on the handle – who knows how these things happen? Maybe an older kid would make us do it. Maybe we would just forget – one moment of carelessness, and *glurrp*, you're stuck, and the teacher has to grab your head and, *rrrrrrip*, there's your little red tongue hanging from the handle. When you're little you believe that evil can somehow reach out and suck you in, so maybe you'd be lured toward that pump – maybe it would speak, 'Hey, kid, c'mere. Stick out your tongue,' and put you in a trance.

Garrison Keillor, from *Lake Wobegon Days*

Some say that ever 'gainst that season comes
Wherein our Saviour's birth is celebrated,
The bird of dawning singeth all night long.
And then, they say, no spirit dare stir abroad,
The nights are wholesome, then no planets strike,
No fairy takes, nor witch hath power to charm,
So hallowed and so gracious is that time.

William Shakespeare, *Hamlet*, Act I, Scene I

A few light taps upon the pane made him turn to the window. It had begun to snow again. He watched sleepily the flakes, silver and dark, falling obliquely against the lamplight. The time had come for him to set out on his journey westward. Yes, the newspapers were right: snow was general all over Ireland. It was falling on every part of the dark central plain, on the treeless hills, falling softly upon the Bog of Allen and, farther westward, softly falling into the dark mutinous Shannon waves. It was falling, too, upon every part of the lonely churchyard on the hill where Michael Furey lay buried. It lay thickly drifted on the crooked crosses and headstones, on the spears of the little gate, on the barren thorns. His soul swooned slowly as he heard the snow falling faintly through the universe and faintly falling, like the descent of their last end, upon all the living and the dead.

James Joyce, from 'The Dead', in *Dubliners*

The Darkling Thrush

I leant upon a coppice gate
  When Frost was spectre-gray,
And Winter's dregs made desolate
  The weakening eye of day.
The tangled bine-stems scored the sky
  Like strings of broken lyres,
And all mankind that haunted nigh
  Had sought their household fires.

The land's sharp features seemed to be
  The Century's corpse outleant,
His crypt the cloudy canopy,
  The wind his death-lament.
The ancient pulse of germ and birth
  Was shrunken hard and dry,
And every spirit upon earth
  Seemed fervourless as I.

At once a voice arose among
  The bleak twigs overhead
In a full-hearted evensong
  Of joy illimited;
An aged thrush, frail, gaunt and small,
  In blast-beruffled plume,

Had chosen thus to fling his soul
    Upon the growing gloom.

So little cause for carolings
    Of such ecstatic sound
Was written on terrestrial things
    Afar or nigh around,
That I could think there trembled through
    His happy good-night air
Some blessed Hope, whereof he knew
    And I was unaware.

            Thomas Hardy, December 1900

Who can be insensible to the outpourings of good feeling and the honeſt interchange of affectionate attachment, which abound at this season of the year? A Chriſtmas family-party! We know nothing in nature more delightful! There seems a magic in the very name of Chriſtmas. Petty jealousies and discords are forgotten: social feelings are awakened in bosoms to which they have long been ſtrangers. Kindly hearts that have yearned towards each other, but have been withheld by false notions of pride and self-dignity, are again reunited, and all is kindness and benevolence! Would that Chriſtmas laſted the whole year through, and that the prejudices and passions which deform our better nature were never called into action among those to whom they should ever be ſtrangers!

Charles Dickens, from 'A Chriſtmas Dinner',
in *Sketches by Boz*

24 DECEMBER: I am a poor man, but I would gladly give ten shillings to find out who sent me the insulting Chriſtmas card I received this morning.

George and Weedon Grossmith,
from *The Diary of a Nobody*

The hares (*Lepus Americanus*) were very familiar. One had her form under my house all winter, separated from me only by the flooring, and she ſtartled me each morning by her haſty departure when I began to ſtir – thump, thump, thump, ſtriking her head againſt the floor timbers in her hurry. They used to come round my door at dusk to nibble the potato parings which I had thrown out, and were so nearly the colour of the ground that they could hardly be diſtinguished when ſtill. Sometimes in the twilight I alternately loſt and recovered sight of one sitting motion-less under my window. When I opened my door in the evening, off they would go with a squeak and a bounce. Near at hand they only excited my pity. One evening one sat by my door two paces from me, at firſt trembling with fear, yet unwilling to move; a poor wee thing, lean and bony, with ragged ears and sharp nose, scant tail and slender paws. It looked as if Nature no longer contained the breed of nobler bloods, but ſtood on her laſt toes. Its large eyes appeared young and unhealthy, almoſt dropsical. I took a ſtep, and lo, away it scud with an elaſtic spring over the snow cruſt, ſtraightening its body and its limbs into grace-ful length, and soon put the foreſt between me and itself – the wild free venison, asserting its vigour and the dignity of Nature. Not without reason was its slenderness. Such then was its nature. (*Lepus, livipes*, lightfoot, some think.)

Henry David Thoreau, from *Walden*

... all seasons shall be sweet to thee,
Whether the summer clothe the general earth
With greenness, or the redbreaſt sit and sing
Betwixt the tufts of snow on the bare branch
Of mossy apple-tree, while the nigh thatch
Smokes in the sun-thaw; whether the eave-drops fall
Heard only in the trances of the blaſt,
Or if the secret miniſtry of froſt
Shall hang them up in silent icicles
Quietly shining to the quiet Moon.

Samuel Taylor Coleridge,
from *Froſt at Midnight*

We are now to feaſt seven ambassadors: Spayne, France,
Poland, Florence and Savoy, besides maskes and much
more; during which time I wold with all my hearte I
were with that noble Ladie of yours, by her turf fire.

Robert Cecil, in a letter to his friend
Lord Shrewsbury, December 1603

The rapid nightfall of mid-December had quite beset the little village as [the Mole and the Rat] approached it on soft feet over a first thin fall of powdery snow. Little was visible but squares of a dusky orange-red on either side of the street, where the firelight or lamplight of each cottage overflowed through the casements into the dark world without. Most of the low latticed windows were innocent of blinds, and to the lookers-in from outside, the inmates, gathered round the tea-table, absorbed in handiwork, or talking with laughter and gesture, had each that happy grace which is the last thing the skilled actor shall capture – the natural grace which goes with perfect unconsciousness of observation. Moving at will from one theatre to another, the two spectators, so far from home themselves, had something of wistfulness in their eyes as they watched a cat being stroked, a sleepy child picked up and huddled off to bed, or a tired man stretch and knock out his pipe on the end of a smouldering log.

But it was from one little window, with its blind drawn down, a mere blank transparency on the night, that the sense of home and the little curtained world within walls – the larger stressful world of outside Nature shut out and forgotten – most pulsated. Close against the white blind hung a bird-cage, clearly silhouetted, every wire, perch and appurtenance distinct and recognisable, even to yesterday's dull-edged lump of sugar. On the middle perch the fluffy occupant, head tucked well into feathers, seemed so near to them as to be easily stroked, had they tried; even the delicate tips of his plumped-out plumage pencilled plainly on the illuminated screen. As they looked, the sleepy little fellow stirred uneasily, woke, shook himself, and raised his head. They could see the gape of his tiny beak as he yawned in a bored sort of way, looked round, and then settled his head into his back again, while the ruffled feathers gradually subsided into perfect stillness. Then a gust of bitter wind took them in the back of the neck, a small sting of frozen sleet on the skin woke them as from a dream, and they knew their toes to be cold and their legs tired, and their own home distant a weary way.

Kenneth Grahame,
from *The Wind in the Willows*

Yesterday in the market there were fresh dates from Elche, the first of the season. They are rather small, treacle-sticky, and come in tortoiseshell-cat colours: black, acorn brown, peeled-chestnut beige; like the lengths of Barcelona corduroy I have bought in the village shop. Inevitably, we were told that the best dates would not be ready until Navidad. That applies to the oranges and the muscatel raisins; and presumably also to the little rosy copper medlars now on sale in the market. They are not yet ripe enough to eat, so I suppose they are to be kept, like Juanita's sister's tomatoes, and the yellow and green Elche melons stored in an esparto basket in the house, for Navidad. We nibble at the candied melon peel in sugar-frosted and lemon-ice-coloured wedges we have bought in the market, and we have already torn open the Christmas-wrapped mazapan (it bears the trade name of El Alce, 'the elk'; a sad-faced moose with tired hooves and snow on its antlers decorates the paper), which is of a kind I have not before encountered.

Elizabeth David
Spectator, 1964

Now winter nights enlarge
   The number of their hours;
And clouds their ſtorms discharge
   Upon the airy towers.
Let now the chimneys blaze
   And cups o'erflow with wine,
Let well-tun'd words amaze
   With harmony divine.
Now yellow waxen lights
   Shall wait on honey Love
While youthful Revels, Masks and Courtly sights,
   Sleep's leaden spells remove.

This time doth well dispense
   With lovers' long discourse;
Much speech hath some defence,
   Though beauty no remorse.
All do not all things well:
   Some measures comely tread;
Some knotted Riddles tell;
   Some poems smoothly read.
The Summer hath his joys,
   And Winter his delights.
Though Love and all his pleasures are but toys,
   They shorten tedious nights.

Thomas Campion

In Sweden St Lucia's Day was formerly marked by some interesting practices. At the first cock-crow, between 1 and 4 a.m., the prettiest girl in the house used to go among the sleeping folk, dressed in a white robe, a red sash, and a wire crown covered with whortleberry twigs and having nine lighted candles fastened in it. She awakened the sleepers and regaled them with a sweet drink or with coffee, sang a special song, and was named 'Lussi' or 'Lussibruden' (Lucy bride). A peculiar feature of the Swedish custom is the presence of lights on Lussi's crown. Lights indeed are the special mark of the festival.

What is the explanation of this feast of lights? There is nothing in the legend of the saint to account for it; her name, however, at once suggests *lux* – light. It is possible that the name gave rise to the special use of lights among the Latin-learned monks who brought Christianity to Sweden, and that the custom spread from them to the common people. A peculiar fitness would be found in it because St Lucia's Day, according to the Old Style, was the shortest day of the year, the turning-point of the sun's light.

Clement A. Miles, from *Christmas in Ritual and Tradition, Christian and Pagan*, 1912

The frost continuing more and more severe, the Thames before London was still planted with booths in formal streets, as in a city or continual fair. All sorts of trades and shops furnished, and full of commodities – even to a printing-press, where the people and ladies took a fancy to have their names printed, and the day and year set down when printed on the Thames. This humour took so universally, that 'twas estimated the printer gained £5 a day, for printing a line only, at sixpence a name, besides what he got by ballads. Coaches now plied from Westminster to the Temple, and from several other stairs to and fro, as in the streets, sleds, sliding with skates, a bull-baiting, horse and coach races, puppet-plays and interludes, cooks, tippling – and lewder places – so that it seemed to be a bacchanalian triumph, or carnival, on the water. It was a severe judgement on the land, for the trees were splitting as if lightning-struck, men and cattle perished in divers places, and the very seas were so locked up with ice that no vessels could stir out or come in. The fowl, fish, and birds, and all our exotic plants and greens, were universally perishing, many parks of deer were destroyed, and all sorts of fuel were so dear that there were great contributions to preserve the poor alive.

John Evelyn's *Diary*, 24 January 1684

If your sleeping place is damp,
   Never mind!
If you wake up with a cramp,
   Never mind!
If your trench should fall in some
Fill your ears and make you dumb
While the sergeant drinks your rum,
   Never mind!

If you have to rise at four,
   Never mind!
If the morning's dark and raw,
   Never mind!
If a duck-board should elope,
And your container has no rope,
And you have to wade and grope,
   Never mind!

Keep a steady upper lip,
   And you'll find,
Every cloud you like to rip
   Silver-lined.
Though the skies are looking grey,
It is ten to one there may
Be a parcel on the way,
   Never mind!

      ' Christmas 1915', Regimental
     Quartermaster-Sergeant E. Clark,
   13th (S) Battalion, the Rifle Brigade

Very faintly, he heard the music again, the same phrase. He swung round vainly searching for it in the air, as if he might see it somewhere like a flickering light.

'Where are you?'

It had gone again. And when he looked back through the window, he saw that his own world had gone with it. In that flash, everything had changed. The snow was there as it had been a moment before, but not piled now on roofs or stretching flat over lawns and fields. There were no roofs, there were no fields. There were only trees. Will was looking out over a great white forest: a forest of massive trees, sturdy as towers and ancient as rock. They were bare of leaves, clad only in the deep snow that lay untouched along every branch, each smallest twig . . .

Will went downstairs to pull on his boots, and the old sheepskin jacket that had belonged, before him, to two or three of his brothers in turn. Then he went out of the back door, closing it quietly behind him, and stood looking out through the quick white vapour of his breath.

The strange white world lay stroked by silence. No birds sang. The garden was no longer there, in this forested land. Nor were the outbuildings nor the old crumbling walls. There lay only a narrow clearing round the house now, hummocked with unbroken snowdrifts, before the trees began, with a narrow path leading away. Will set out down the white tunnel of the path, slowly,

Stepping high to keep the snow out of his boots. As soon as he moved away from the house, he felt very much alone, and he made himself go on without looking back over his shoulder, because he knew that when he looked, he would find that the house was gone.

Susan Cooper, from *The Dark is Rising*

Thursday, June 22—MIDWINTER. The sun reached its maximum depression at about 2.30 P.M. on the 22nd, Greenwich Mean Time: this is 2.30 A.M. on the 23rd according to the local time of the 180th meridian which we are keeping. Dinner tonight is therefore the meal which is nearest the sun's critical change of course, and has been observed with all the festivity customary at Xmas at home.

Whilst revelry was the order of the day in our hut, the elements without seemed desirous of celebrating the occasion with equal emphasis and greater decorum. The eastern sky was massed with swaying auroral light, the most vivid and beautiful display that I had ever seen–fold on fold the arches and curtains of vibrating luminosity rose and spread across the sky, to slowly fade and yet again spring to glowing life. It is impossible to witness such a beautiful phenomenon without a sense of awe … To the little silent group which stood at gaze before such enchantment it seemed profane to return to the mental and physical atmosphere of our house. Finally when I stepped within, I was glad to find that there had been a gentle movement bedwards, and in the next half hour the last of the roisterers had succumbed to slumber.

Captain R. F. Scott, from *Scott's Last Expedition*, *the Journals of Captain R. F. Scott*

This King lay royally at Camelot at Christmas tide with many fine lords, the best of men, all the rich brethren of the Round Table, with right rich revel and careless mirth. There full many heroes journeyed betimes, jousted full gaily; then returned these gentle knights to the court to make carols. For there the feast was held full fifteen days alike with all the meat and the mirth that men could devise. Such a merry tumult, glorious to hear; joyful din by day, dancing at night. All was high joy in halls and chambers with lords and ladies as pleased them best. With all the weal in the world they dwelt there together, the most famous knights save only Christ, the loveliest ladies that ever had life, and he, the comeliest of kings, who holds the court. For all this fair company were in their prime in the hall, the happiest troop under heaven with the proudest of kings. Truly it would be hard to name anywhere so brave a band.

From *Sir Gawain and the Green Knight*,
translated by K.G.T. Webster

Mr. Hobbs told me that the cause of his Lordship's [Francis Bacon] death was trying an Experiment; viz. as he was taking the aire in a Coach with Dr. Witherborne (a Scotchman, Physitian to the King) towards Highgate, snow lay on the ground, and it came into my Lord's thoughts, why flesh might not be preserved in snow, as in Salt. They were resolved they would try the Experiment presently. They alighted out of the Coach and went into a poore woman's house at the bottom of Highgate hill, and bought a Hen, and made the woman exenterate it, and then stuffed the body with Snow, and my Lord did help to doe it himselfe. The Snow so chilled him that he immediately fell so extremely ill, that he could not returne to his Lodging (I suppose then at Graye's Inne) but went to the Earl of Arundel's house at High-gate, where they putt him into a good bed warmed with a Panne, but it was a damp bed that had not been layne-in about a yeare before, which gave him such a colde that in 2 or 3 dayes as I remember Mr. Hobbes told me, he dyed of Suffocation.

John Aubrey, from *Brief Lives*

An excellent way to keep fresh meat during the winter is practiced by the farmers in the country, which they term 'salting in snow'. Take a large clean tub, cover the bottom three or four inches thick with clean snow; then lay pieces of fresh meat, spare ribs, fowls, or whatever you wish to keep, and cover each layer with two or three inches of snow, taking particular care to fill snow into every cranny and crevice between the pieces, and around the edge of the tub. Fowl must also be filled inside with the snow. When the tub is filled, the last layer must be snow, pressed down tight; then cover the tub, which must be kept in a cold place, the colder the better. The meat will not freeze, and unless there happen to be a long spell of warm weather, the snow will not thaw, but the meat remain as fresh and juicy when it is taken out to be cooked, as when it was first killed.

Sarah Josepha Hale,
from *The Good Housekeeper*, 1841

Blackbirds and Thrushes, particularly the former, feed in hard winters upon the shell snail horns by hunting them from the hedge bottoms and wood ſtulps and taking them to a ſtone where they brake them in a very dexterous manner. Any curious observer of nature may see in hard froſts the shells of pootys [snails] thickly littered round a ſtone in the lanes, and if he waits a short time he will quickly see one of these birds coming with a snailhorn in his bill which he conſtantly taps on the ſtone till it is broken. He then extraƈts the snail and like a true sportsman eagerly haſtens to hunt them again in the hedges or woods where a frequent ruſtle of their little feet is heard among the dead leaves.

John Clare, from a letter, 21 April 1825

London Snow

When men were all asleep the snow came flying,
In large white flakes falling on the city brown,
Stealthily and perpetually settling and loosely lying,
    Hushing the latest traffic of the drowsy town;
Deadening, muffling, stifling its murmurs failing;
Lazily and incessantly floating down and down:
    Silently sifting and veiling road, roof and railing;
Hiding difference, making unevenness even,
Into angles and crevices softly drifting and sailing.
    All night it fell, and when full inches seven
It lay in the depth of its uncompacted lightness,
The clouds blew off from a high and frosty heaven;
    And all woke earlier for the unaccustomed
      brightness
Of the winter dawning, the strange unheavenly glare:
The eye marvelled – marvelled at the dazzling
    whiteness;
    The ear hearkened to the stillness of the solemn air;
No sound of wheel rumbling nor of foot falling,
And the busy morning cries came thin and spare.
    Then boys I heard, as they went to school, calling,
They gathered up the crystal manna to freeze
Their tongues with tasting, their hands with
    snowballing;

Or rioted in a drift, plunging up to the knees;
Or peering up from under the white-mossed wonder,
'O look at the trees!' they cried, 'O look at the trees!'

With lessened load a few carts creak and blunder,
Following along the white deserted way,
A country company long dispersed asunder:

When now already the sun, in pale display
Standing by Paul's high dome, spread forth below
His sparkling beams, and awoke the ſtir of the day.

For now doors open, and war is waged with the snow;
And trains of sombre men, paſt tale of number,
Tread long brown paths, as toward their toil they go:

But even for them awhile no cares encumber
Their minds diverted; the daily word is unspoken,
The daily thoughts of labour and sorrow slumber
At the sight of the beauty that greets them, for the
    charm they have broken.

Robert Bridges

What [Professor Parkins] saw was this:

A long ſtretch of shore – shingle edged by sand, and interſected at short intervals with black groynes running down to the water – a scene, in fact, so like that of his afternoon's walk that, in the absence of any landmark, it could not be diſtinguished therefrom. The light was obscure, conveying an impression of gathering ſtorm, late winter evening, and slight cold rain. On this bleak ſtage at firſt no actor was visible. Then, in the distance, a bobbing black object appeared; a moment more, and it was a man running, jumping, clambering over the groynes, and every few seconds looking eagerly back. The nearer he came the more obvious it was that he was not only anxious, but even terribly frightened, though his face was not to be diſtinguished. He was, moreover, almoſt at the end of his ſtrength. On he came; each successive obſtacle seemed to cause him more difficulty than the laſt. 'Will he get over the next one?' thought Parkins; 'it seems a little higher than the others.' Yes; half climbing, half throwing himself, he did get over, and fell all in a heap on the other side (the side neareſt to the spectator). There, as if really unable to get up again, he remained crouching under the groyne, looking up in an attitude of painful anxiety.

So far no cause whatever for the fear of the runner had been shown; but now there began to be seen, far up the shore, a little flicker of something light-coloured

37

moving to and fro with great swiftness and irregularity. Rapidly growing larger, it, too, declared itself as a figure in pale, fluttering draperies, ill-defined. There was something about its motion which made Parkins very unwilling to see it at close quarters. It would ſtop, raise arms, bow itself toward the sand, then run ſtooping across the beach to the water-edge and back again; and then, rising upright, once more continue its course forward at a speed that was ſtartling and terrifying. The moment came when the pursuer was hovering about from left to right only a few yards beyond the groyne where the runner lay in hiding. After two or three ineffectual caſtings hither and thither it came to a ſtop, ſtood upright, with arms raised high, and then darted ſtraight forward towards the groyne . . .

M. R. James, from 'Oh, Whiſtle, and I'll Come to You, My Lad'

I, singularly moved
To love the lovely that are not beloved,
Of all the Seasons, most
Love Winter, and to trace
The sense of the Trophonian pallor on her face.
It is not death, but plenitude of peace;
And the dim cloud that does the world enfold
Hath less the characters of dark and cold
Than warmth and light asleep,
And correspondent breathing seems to keep
With the infant harvest, breathing soft below
Its eider coverlet of snow.

Coventry Patmore, from 'Winter'

An axe-age, a sword-age, shields will be gashed: there will be a wind-age and a wolf-age before the world is wrecked.

First of all Midgard will be wrenched and racked by wars for three winters. Fathers will slaughter sons; brothers will be drenched in one another's blood, mothers will desert their menfolk and seduce their own sons; brothers will bed with sisters.

Then Fimbulvetr, the winter of winters, will grip and throttle Midgard. Driving snow clouds will converge from north and south and east and west. There will be bitter frosts, biting winds; the shining sun will be helpless. Three such winters will follow each other with no summers between them.

So the end will begin. Then the children of the old giantess in Iron Wood will have their say: the wolf Skoll will seize the sun between his jaws and swallow her – he will spatter Asgard with gore; and his brother Hati will catch the moon and mangle him. The stars will vanish from the sky.

From 'Ragnarok', *The Norse Myths*, retold by Kevin Crossley-Holland

25 December 1940: Christmas Day! Today has been of the happiest, not because of the 'highlights', but because of the absence of the 'highlights'. No lengthy wireless bulletins, but just the reassurance that there were no enemy aircraft over the country! No getting up and journeying into town before dawn, but waking up at 10 and Mother coming into the room. We hugged, she saying 'Thank God for another Christmas Day!' and I 'Thank God we have a roof over our heads.' Mother went down the stair to wish Mrs Stewart a happy Christmas day and found her cooking for 16 soldiers whom she had invited to breakfast.

As long as we have a peaceful Christmas Day there is hope for this civilisation of ours. Today has been a lovely experience.

Pam Ashford, from her diary for
the Mass Observation Project

The weeks around Christmas were always fine and sunny. The violets were in flower on the banks, and a little white plant like candytuft. The usual windless calm prevailed. Then the women went out to the olive groves to pick the last crop of the year, and before long the cold winds and rain that marked our two months' winter began. In the streets below my house the ivy came into flower and every time I went out in the sunshine I smelt it.

Gerald Brenan, from *South from Granada:*
Seven Years in an Andalusian Village, 1957

Sunday, Christmas Day, 1870: As I lay awake praying in the early morning, I thought I heard a sound of distant bells. It was an intense frost. I sat down in my bath upon a sheet of thick ice which broke in the middle into large pieces whilst sharp points and jagged edges stuck all round the sides of the tub like chevaux de frises, not particularly comforting to the naked thighs and loins, for the keen ice cut like broken glass. The ice water stung and scorched like fire. I had to collect the floating pieces of ice and pile them on a chair before I could use the sponge in my hands for it was a mass of ice. The morning was most brilliant . . .

Reverend Francis Kilvert, from his Diary

When icicles hang by the wall,
   And Dick the shepherd blows his nail,
And Tom bears logs into the hall,
   And milk comes frozen home in pail,
When blood is nipped and ways be foul,
   Then nightly sings the staring owl,
      Tu-whit, Tu-who!
   A merry note,
While greasy Joan doth keel the pot.

When all aloud the wind doth blow,
   And coughing drowns the parson's saw,
And bird sits brooding in the snow,
   And Marian's nose looks red and raw,
When roasted crabs hiss in the bowl,
   Then nightly sings the staring owl,
      Tu-whit, Tu-who!
   A merry note,
While greasy Joan doth keel the pot.

William Shakespeare, from
Love's Labour's Lost, Act V Scene II

A North London garden. Winter. A spot of cerise, grey and black, in an old pear tree. I am standing at the window, there is snow on the ground. A cock bullfinch. A sporadic winter visitor to outlying city gardens: not unusual. Looking for clematis or forsythia buds; or honeysuckle berries. A week ago, in Dorset, I counted twenty-seven cock bullfinches in a grove of bullace. The bullace in blossom. Bullace jam. 'Whistling' bullfinch – I could do it as a boy. A Devonshire combe and our cottage there. Waking up and hearing the whistles very close and looking out and seeing six cock bullfinches sitting in the first sunlight on an apple tree. That apple tree, with its yellow-green, smoky-tasting apples no one ever knew the name of. That same bullace grove in summer. I lie in the shade there and a bullfinch sings overhead: its strange, monotonous little five-note fluting chant. Like Webern. Like a last cardinal, in the freezing wind on the dying pear tree. The future, a jet heading for Heathrow, whines over. I feel depressed. I have a busy day I don't want ahead. I hate cities, and summer will never come again. The bullfinch drops down into the garden. A flash of white rump. Then nothing. I can't see it anymore. A squirt of green memories, like a brief taste on the tongue. But enough to keep me going, the bitter and dull day through.

John Fowles, from his essay 'The Blinded Eye', 1971

The time draws near the birth of Christ:
    The moon is hid; the night is still;
    The Christmas bells from hill to hill
Answer each other in the mist.

Four voices of four hamlets round,
    From far and near, on mead and moor,
    Swell out and fail, as if a door
Were shut between me and the sound:

Each voice four changes on the wind,
    That now dilate, and now decrease,
    Peace and goodwill, goodwill and peace,
Peace and goodwill, to all mankind.

This year I slept and woke with pain,
    And almost wished no more to wake,
    And that my hold on life would break
Before I heard those bells again:

But they my troubled spirit rule,
    For they controlled me when a boy;
    They bring me sorrow touched with joy,
The merry merry bells of Yule.

Alfred, Lord Tennyson,
from *In Memoriam*

The common assumption made in our temperate climes that Russian sledges, drawn by swift horses, skim smoothly over the snow as though crossing a frozen lake, has given us a rather agreeable idea of sledging as a method of travel. The truth is very different . . . Imagine a metal box, hermetically sealed yet subtly penetrable by the fine snow, which seeps in, powdering your face white. Imagine yourself shaken about in it, violently and almost without pause, rather as shot is shaken in a bottle to clean it. Imagine the resultant sharp contact with the casing of the sled. Imagine, on top of all that, a general sensation of malaise plus a powerful desire to vomit, which can fairly be called snow-sickness, from its strong resemblance to the state known to travellers by sea.

Hector Berlioz, from *The Memoirs of Hector Berlioz*

Once upon a time – of all the good days in the year, on Chriſtmas Eve – old Scrooge sat busy in his counting-house. It was cold, bleak, biting weather; foggy withal: and he could hear the people in the court outside go wheezing up and down, beating their hands upon their breaſts, and ſtamping their feet upon the pavement ſtones to warm them. The city clocks had only juſt gone three, but it was quite dark already – it had not been light all day – and candles were flaring in the windows of the neighbouring offices, like ruddy smears upon the palp-able brown air. The fog came pouring in at every chink and keyhole, and was so dense without, that although the court was of the narroweſt, the houses opposite were mere phantoms. To see the dingy cloud come drooping down, obscuring everything, one might have thought that Nature lived hard by, and was brewing on a large scale.

The door of Scrooge's counting-house was open that he might keep his eye upon his clerk, who in a dismal little cell beyond, a sort of tank, was copying letters. Scrooge had a very small fire, but the clerk's fire was so very much smaller that it looked like one coal. But he couldn't replenish it, for Scrooge kept the coal-box in his own room; and so surely as the clerk came in with the shovel, the maſter predicted that it would be necessary for them to part. Wherefore the clerk put on his white comforter, and tried to warm himself at the candle; in which effort, not being a man of strong imagination, he failed.

'A Merry Christmas, uncle! God save you!' cried a cheerful voice. It was the voice of Scrooge's nephew, who came upon him so quickly that this was the first intimation he had of his approach.

'Bah!' said Scrooge. 'Humbug!'

Charles Dickens, from *A Christmas Carol*

Every snowflake has an infinite beauty which is enhanced by knowledge that the investigator will, in all probability, never find another exactly like it. Consequently, photographing these transient forms of Nature gives to the worker something of the spirit of a discoverer. The photographing of snowflakes, although quite delicate work, can hardly be called difficult, although some hardships attend it, because the work must all be done in a temperature below freezing and under conditions of much physical exposure.

The necessary accessories are an observation microscope, a pair of thick mittens, microscope slides, a sharp-pointed wooden splint, a feather and a turkey wing or similar duster; also, an extra focussing back for the camera with a magnifying lens attached. A blackboard with stiff wire or metal handles at the ends, so that the hands will not touch and warm it, is used to collect the specimens.

The snowflakes are caught on the blackboard as they fall and examined by the naked eye or with a hand magnifying glass. The feather duster is used to brush the board clean until two or more promising specimens alight upon it, when it is immediately removed indoors. From this point onward the photographer must work fast and care be taken not to breathe on the crystals . . .

Wilson 'Snowflake' Bentley, from
'Photographing Snowflakes'

Storm and destruction shattering
    Strike fear upon the world,
The winds are out, and through high heaven
    Their Bacchanals are hurled.
Their league is broken, burst the girth,
And launched their fury on the earth,

Torrent on torrent falls the rain.
    Dark are the lovely Pleiades,
Their seven lamps are out, and dark
    The Houses where abide the stars.
The Sirius shines no more at all,
And heaven is hung with blackest pall.

Yet through the summits of the sky
    Flashes afar the livid Levin,
And cataracts of pallid fire
    Pour from the toppling crests of heaven.
Struggling with clouds the mountains stand,
    The dark sea masses on the strand,
Following wave on wave behind
The rush and ruin of the wind.

A Scholar of Malmesbury (8th century)

There was the smell of hot toast and ale from the kitchen, at the breakfast hour; the favourite anthem, the green boughs, and the short sermon, gave the appropriate festal character to the church-going; and aunt and uncle Moss, with all their seven children, were looking like so many reflectors of the bright parlour fire, when the church-goers came back, stamping the snow from their feet. The plum-pudding was of the same handsome roundness as ever, and came in with the symbolic blue flames around it, as if it had been heroically snatched from the nether fires into which it had been thrown by dyspeptic Puritans; the dessert was as splendid as ever, with its golden oranges, brown nuts, and the crystalline light and dark of apple jelly and damson cheese: in all these things Christmas was as it had always been since Tom could remember; it was only distinguished, if by anything, by superior sliding and snowballs.

George Eliot, *The Mill on the Floss*

I cannot possibly describe all the sufferings, anguish, and scenes of desolation I had seen and passed through, nor those which I was fated ſtill to see and endure; they left deep and terrible memories, which I have never forgotten.

This was 25 November, perhaps about seven o'clock in the morning, and as yet it was hardly light. I was musing on all I had seen, when the head of the column appeared. Those in advance seemed to be Generals, a few on horseback, but the greater part on foot. There were also a great number of other officers, the remnant of the Doomed Squadron and Battalion formed on the 22nd, and barely exiſting at the end of three days. Those on foot dragged themselves painfully along, almoſt all of them having the feet frozen and wrapped in rags or in bits of sheepskin, and all nearly dying of hunger. Afterwards came the small remains of the Cavalry of the Guard. The Emperor came next, on foot, and carrying a ſtick. He wore a large cloak lined with fur, a dark-red velvet cap with black fox fur on his head. Murat walked on foot at his right, and on his left Prince Eugene, Viceroy of Italy. Next came the Marshals, Berthier – Prince of Neufchatel – Ney, Mortier, Lefebvre, with other Marshals and Generals whose corps had been nearly annihilated.

The Emperor mounted a horse as soon as he passed: so did a few of those with him, the greater part of them having no more horses to ride. Seven or eight hundred officers and non-commissioned officers followed, walking in order and perfect silence, and carrying the eagles of their different regiments, which so often had led them to victory. This was all that remained of 60,000 men.

From *The Retreat from Moscow: The Memoirs of Sergeant Bourgogne* (*1812–13*), translated by J. W. Fortescue

Napoleon

'What is the world, O soldiers?
    It is I:
I, this incessant snow,
    This northern sky;
Soldiers, this solitude
    Through which we go
        Is I.'

Walter de la Mare

Christmas cards are a nightmare to me, all under-stamped so I've never paid less than 1/- each. Like you, I have dozens from totally unknown people, in some cases bearing photographs of their totally unknown faces & those of their T.U. children to boot. But I forget people very soon so this means nothing & I can see from the fervid messages that once we have been very intimate.

Nancy Mitford, from a letter to Evelyn Waugh,
29 December 1950

It is winter proper; the cold weather, such as it is, has come to stay. I bloom indoors like a forced forsythia; I come in to come out. At night I read and write, and things I have never understood become clear; I reap the harvest of the rest of the year's planting.

Annie Dillard, from
Pilgrim at Tinker Creek

Then there was quite a long story about two undergraduates spending Christmas in a country house that belonged to one of them. An uncle, next heir to the estate, lived near. Plausible and learned Roman priest, living with the uncle, makes himself agreeable to the young men. Dark walks home at night after dining with the uncle. Curious disturbances as they pass through the shrubberies. Strange, shapeless tracks in the snow round the house, observed in the morning. Efforts to lure away the companion and isolate the proprietor and get him to come out after dark. Ultimate defeat and death of the priest, upon whom the Familiar, baulked of another victim, turns.

There may be possibilities, too, in the Christmas cracker, if the right people pull it, and if the motto which they find inside has the right message on it. They will probably leave the party early, pleading indisposition; but very likely a previous engagement of long standing would be the more truthful excuse.

M. R. James, from 'Stories I
Have Tried to Write'

The walls are of red sandstone, dressed into long rect-angles, with a tall sentry-like buttress in each corner to support the corbelled roof. The passage to the outside world is at the base of one wall. Set waist-high into the other three are square openings into cells which disap-pear into the darkness of the walls. That's where they laid the dead, once the bones had been cleaned of flesh by weather and birds. The stone blocks which would once have sealed these graves lie on the gravel floor. And the point is, the ancients who built this tomb orientated it precisely: the long passageway faces exactly the set-ting midwinter sun. Consequently, for the few days around the winter solstice a beam of the setting sun shines along the passage, and onto the tomb's back wall. In recent years, people have crept along the passageway at midwinter to witness this, the complicit kiss. Some, apparently, find it overwhelming.

Kathleen Jamie, a description of Maes Howe,
from her essay 'Darkness and Light',
published in *Findings*

Winter Sports

The ice upon our pond's so thin
That poor Mamma has fallen in!
We cannot reach her from the shore
Until the surface freezes more.
Ah me, my heart grows weary waiting –
Besides, I want to have some skating.

Harry Graham, from
Ruthless Rhymes for Heartless Homes

The Polar Bear

The Polar Bear is unaware
  Of cold that cuts me through:
For why? He has a coat of hair.
  I wish I had one too!

Hilaire Belloc

Bring out the tall tales now that we told by the fire as the gaslight bubbled like a diver. Ghosts whooed like owls in the long nights when I dared not look over my shoulder; animals lurked in the cubbyhole under the stairs where the gas meter ticked. And I remember that we went singing carols once, when there wasn't the shaving of a moon to light the flying streets. At the end of a long road was a drive that led to a large house, and we stumbled up the darkness of the drive that night, each one of us afraid, each one holding a stone in his hand in case, and all of us too brave to say a word. The wind through the trees made noises as of old and unpleasant and maybe webfooted men wheezing in caves. We reached the black bulk of the house.

'What shall we give them? Hark the Herald?'

'No,' Jack said, 'Good King Wenceslas. I'll count three.'

One, two, three, and we began to sing, our voices high and seemingly distant in the snow-felted darkness round the house that was occupied by nobody we knew. We stood close together, near the dark door.

Good King Wenceslas looked out
On the Feast of Stephen . . .

And then a small, dry voice, like the voice of someone who has not spoken for a long time, joined our singing: a small, dry, eggshell voice from the other side of the door: a small dry voice through the keyhole. And when we stopped running we were outside *our* house; the front room was lovely; balloons floated under the hot-water-bottle-gulping gas; everything was good again and shone over the town.

'Perhaps it was a ghost,' Jim said.

'Perhaps it was trolls,' Dan said, who was always reading.

'Let's go in and see if there's any jelly left,' Jack said. And we did that.

Dylan Thomas, from *A Child's Christmas in Wales*

On winter evenings when the mist hangs low
Over the reed-beds and the reeds look blue
And chill, chill, chill
          The wild ducks call each other,
I shall remember you.

Anonymous (5th or 6th-century Japanese),
translated by Graeme Wilson

Before the snow comes sleet,
And wind from out the East.
One moment may let slip
Our goodly fellowship.
Death clutches at our feet.
Who knows when next we meet?
Yet still the wine is sweet.
O King, enjoy the feast!

Anon, 780 BC, from *Lyrics from the Chinese*,
translated by Helen Waddell

February: A spell of fine soft weather. I wander about a good deal, sometimes at night under the moon. Tonight took a long look at the President's house. The white portico – the palace-like, tall, round columns, spotless as snow – the walls also – the tender and soft moonlight, flooding the pale marble, and making peculiar faint languishing shades, not shadows – everywhere a soft transparent hazy, thin, blue moon-lace, hanging in the air – the brilliant and extra-plentiful clusters of gas, on and around the façade, columns, portico, etc – everything so white, so marbly pure and dazzling, yet soft – the White House of future poems, and of dreams and dramas, there in the soft and copious moon – the gorgeous front, in the trees, under the lustrous flooding moon, full of reality, full of illusion – the forms of the trees, leafless, silent, in trunk and myriad angles of branches, under the stars and sky – the White House of the land, and of beauty and night – sentries at the gates, and by the portico, silent, pacing there in blue overcoats – stopping you not at all, but eyeing you with sharp eyes, whichever way you move . . .

Walt Whitman, from *Specimen Days in America*

The Mistletoe Bough

The mistletoe hung in the castle hall;
The holly branch shone on the old oak wall,
The Baron's retainers were blithe and gay;
Keeping the Christmas holiday.

The Baron beheld with a father's pride
His beautiful child, Lord Lovell's bride.
While she, with her bright eyes, seemed to be
The star of that goodly company.
Oh, the mistletoe bough,
Oh, the mistletoe bough.

'I'm weary of dancing, now,' she cried;
'Here, tarry a moment, I'll hide, I'll hide,
And, Lovell, be sure you're the first to trace
The clue to my secret lurking place.'

Away she ran, and her friends began
Each tower to search and each nook to scan.
And young Lovell cried, 'Oh, where dost thou hide?
I'm alone without you, my own dear bride.'

They sought her that night, they sought her next day,
They sought her in vain when a week passed away.
In the highest, the lowest, the loneliest spot,
Young Lovell sought wildly, but found her not.

And years flew by, and their grief at last
Was told as a sorrowful tale long past;
And when Lovell appear'd the children cried,
'See the old man weeps for his fairy bride.'

At length an old chest that had long lain hid
Was found in the castle; they raised the lid.
And a skeleton form lay mouldering there
In the bridal wreath of that lady fair.

Oh, sad was her fate! – in sportive jest
She hid from her lord in the old oak chest,
It closed with a spring! And dreadful doom,
The bride lay clasp'd in a living tomb.
Oh, the mistletoe bough,
Oh, the mistletoe bough.

                                        Thomas Haynes Bayly

We came up to take over the trenches on the front between Frelinghien and Houplines, where our regiment and the Scottish Seaforth Highlanders were face to face. It was a cold ſtarry night and the Scots were a hundred or so metres in front of us in their trenches where, as we discovered, like us they were up to their knees in mud . . .

Suddenly, for no apparent reason, our enemies began to fire on our lines. Our soldiers had hung little Chriſtmas trees covered with candles above the trenches and our enemies, seeing the lights, thought we were about to launch a surprise attack. But, by midnight it was calm once more. Next morning the miſt was slow to clear and suddenly my orderly threw himself into my dugout to say that both the German and Scottish soldiers had come out of their trenches and were fraternising along the front. I grabbed my binoculars and looking cautiously over the parapet saw the incredible sight of our soldiers exchanging cigarettes, schnapps and chocolate with the enemy. Later a Scottish soldier appeared with a football which seemed to come from nowhere and a few minutes later a real football match got underway. The Scots marked their goal mouth with their ſtrange caps and we did the same with ours. It was far from easy to play on the frozen ground, but we continued, keeping rigorously to the rules, despite the faɛt that it only laſted an hour and that we had no referee. A great many of the passes went wide, but all the amateur footballers, although they must have been very tired, played with huge enthusiasm. Us Germans really roared when a gust of wind revealed that the Scots wore no drawers under their kilts – and hooted and whistled every time they caught an impudent glimpse of one of the posteriors belonging to one of 'yesterday's enemies' . . .

The game finished with a score of three goals to two in favour of Fritz against Tommy.

Leutnant Johannes Niemann, of the
133rd Royal Saxon Regiment

Yf that the daye,
    Of S. Paule be cheare
Than shall betide,
    an happy yere.
Yf it do chaunce,
    to snowe or rayne
Than shall be deare,
    all kynde of grayne.
But and the wynde,
    than be a lofte
Warres shall vexe,
    this Realme full ofte.
And yf the Clowdes
    make darke the sky
Both Neate and Fowle
    that yeare shall dye.

Erra Pater, from
The Progno∫tycacion for Ever, 1540

First Sight

Lambs that learn to walk in snow
When their bleating clouds the air
Meet a vast unwelcome, know
Nothing but a sunless glare.
Newly stumbling to and fro
All they find, outside the fold,
Is a wretched width of cold.

As they wait beside the ewe,
Her fleeces wetly caked, there lies
Hidden round them, waiting too,
Earth's immeasurable surprise.
They could not grasp it if they knew,
What so soon will wake and grow
Utterly unlike the snow.

Philip Larkin

The walls of the palace were formed of the drifting snow, and the windows and doors of the cutting winds. There were more than a hundred halls, all blown together by the snow: the greateſt of these extended for several miles; the ſtrong Northern Lights illumined them all, and how great and empty, how icily cold and shining they all were! Never was merriment there, not even a little bears' ball, at which the ſtorm could have played the music, while the bears walked about on their hind legs and showed off their pretty manners; never any little coffee gossip among the young lady white foxes. Empty, vaſt and cold were the halls of the Snow Queen. In the midſt of this immense empty snow hall was a frozen lake, which had burſt into a thousand pieces; but each piece was like the reſt, so that it was a perfeċt work of art; and in the middle of the lake sat the Snow Queen when she was at home, and then she said that she sat in the mirror of reason, and that this was the only one, and the beſt in the world.

Hans Chriſtian Andersen,
from 'The Snow Queen'

Carol Singing

I had almost forgotten the singing in the streets,
Snow piled up by the houses, drifting
Underneath the door into the warm room,
Firelight, lamplight, the little lame cat
Dreaming in soft sleep on the hearth, mother dozing,
Waiting for Christmas to come, the boys and me
Trudging over blanket fields waving lanterns to the
    sky.
I had almost forgotten the smell, the feel of it all,
The coming back home, with girls laughing like stars,
Their cheeks, holly berries, me kissing one,
Silent-tongued, soberly, by the long church wall;
Then back to the kitchen table, supper on the white
    cloth,
Cheese, bread, the home-made wine:
Symbols of the Night's joy, a holy feast.
And I wonder now, years gone, mother gone,
The boys and girls scattered, drifted away with the
    snowflakes,
Lamplight done, firelight over,
If the sounds of our singing in the streets are still
    there,
Those old tunes, still praising:
And now, a life-time of Decembers away from it all,

A branch of remembering holly spears my cheeks,
And I think it may be so;
Yes, I believe it may be so.

Leonard Clark

In trench warfare five things are important: firewood, food, tobacco, candles, and the enemy. In winter on the Zaragoza front they were important in that order, with the enemy a bad last. Except at night, when a surprise-attack was always conceivable, nobody bothered with the enemy. They were simply remote black insects whom one occasionally saw hopping to and fro. The real preoccupation of both armies was trying to keep warm . . .

Often I used to gaze round the wintry landscape and marvel at the futility of it all. The inconclusiveness of such a kind of war! Earlier, about October, there had been savage fighting for all these hills; then, because the lack of men and arms, especially artillery, made any large-scale operation impossible, each army had dug itself in and settled down on the hill-tops it had won. The scenery was stupendous, if you could forget that every mountain-top was occupied by troops and was therefore littered with tin cans and crusted with dung. To the right of us the sierra bent south-eastwards and made way for the wide, veined valley that stretched across to Huesca. In the middle of the plain a few tiny cubes sprawled like a throw of the dice; this was the town of Robres, which was in Loyalist possession. Often in the mornings the valley was hidden under seas of cloud, out of which the hills rose flat and blue, giving the landscape a strange resemblance to a photographic negative. Beyond Huesca there were more hills of the same formation as our own, streaked with a pattern of snow which altered day by day. In the far distance the monstrous peaks of the Pyrenees, where the snow never melts, seemed to float upon nothing. Even down in the plain everything looked dead and bare. The hills opposite us were grey and wrinkled like the skins of elephants. Almost always the sky was empty of birds. I do not think I have ever seen a country where there were so few birds . . .

George Orwell, from
Homage to Catalonia

For winter's rains and ruins are over,
    And all the season of snows and sins;
The days dividing lover and lover,
    The light that loses, the night that wins;
And time remembered is grief forgotten,
And frosts are slain and flowers begotten,
And in green underwood and cover
    Blossom by blossom the spring begins.

Algernon Charles Swinburne,
from *Atalanta in Calydon*

January is Nature's spoilt-child: all her gifts are laid under contribution by a cook of genius. Beef, veal, mutton, port, venison, hare, pheasant, plover, the black cock, partridge, wild goose, duck, woodcock, &c., troop up to the great city, dead or alive; and in battalions that serve only to entrance with delight the assembled forces of *bon-vivants*, to whom gold will render them an easy and immediate sacrifice. Cauliflowers and celery rear their tender and delicately juicy heads, merely for the pleasure of being decapitated. At this period, truffles are poetry. And now it is, that a householder must either give good and frequent dinners, or permit himself to be thrown without the pale of society, with, to use an animating figure, the pitchfork of universal resentment. When the appetite is both excellent and discriminating, the dinner must be abundant and admirable, – anything short of these qualities is at all times a fault, but, in January, it is a moral assassination!

Talk not to me about presents at this time of the year: there are gifts which are to be valued more than gold, silver, or precious stones, – I mean good dinners.

From *Gunter's Confectioner's Oracle*, 1830

The Snowdrop

Many, many welcomes,
February fair-maid,
Ever as of old time,
Solitary firstling,
Coming in the cold time,
Prophet of the gay time,
Prophet of the May time,
Prophet of the roses,
Many, many welcomes,
February fair-maid!

Alfred, Lord Tennyson

It is well ascertained that the Tartars date the commencement of their year from the month of February, and on that occasion it is customary for the grand khan, as well as all who are subject to him, in their several countries, to clothe themselves in white garments, which, according to their ideas, are the emblem of good fortune; and they assume this dress at the beginning of the year, in the hope that, during the whole course of it, nothing but what is fortunate may happen to them, and that they may enjoy pleasure and comfort. Upon this day the inhabitants of all the provinces and kingdoms who hold land or rights of jurisdiction under the grand khan, send him valuable presents of gold, silver and precious stones, together with many pieces of white cloth, which they add, with the intent that his majesty may experience throughout the year uninterrupted felicity, and possess treasures adequate to all his expenses. With the same view, the nobles, princes and all ranks of the community, make reciprocal presents, at their respective houses, of white articles; embracing each other with demonstrations of joy and festivity, and saying, 'May good fortune attend you through the coming year and may everything you undertake succeed to your wish.' On this occasion great numbers of beautiful white horses are presented to the grand khan; or if not perfectly white, it is at least the prevailing colour. On this day it is that all his elephants, amounting to five thousand, are exhibited in procession, covered with housings of cloth, fancifully and richly worked with gold and silk, in figures of birds and beasts. Each of these supports upon its shoulders two coffers filled with vessels of plate and other apparatus for the use of the court. Then follows a train of camels, in like manner laden with various necessary articles of furniture. When the whole are properly arranged, they pass in review before his majesty, and form a pleasing spectacle.

From *The Travels of Marco Polo*,
translated by William Marsden

20th January 1798: The green paths down the hill-sides are channels for streams. The young wheat is streaked by silver lines of water running between the ridges, the sheep are gathered together on the slopes. After the wet dark days, the country seems more populous. It peoples itself in the sunbeams.

Dorothy Wordsworth,
from *The Alfoxden Journal*

Thaw

Over the land freckled with snow half-thawed
The speculating rooks at their nests cawed
And saw from elm-tops, delicate as flower of grass,
What we below could not see, Winter pass.

Edward Thomas

List of authors

Acknowledgements

Thanks to Kevin Crossley-Holland for permission to use an extract from 'Ragnarok', from *The Norse Myths* (1980); Susan Cooper for an extract from *The Dark is Rising* (1984); Kathleen Jamie and Sort of Books for an extract from *Findings* by Kathleen Jamie © Kathleen Jamie 2005; 'First Sight' by Philip Larkin, from *The Whitsun Weddings* © The Estate of Philip Larkin, 1988, 2003. Permission of Faber and Faber Ltd and The Estate of Philip Larkin; 'A 14-Year-Old Convalescent Cat in the Winter' by Gavin Ewart, from *The New Ewart: Poems 1980–1982* © The Estate of Gavin Ewart 1982. Reprinted by permission of Hutchinson and the Estate of Gavin Ewart.